PERSIAN SCRIPT HACKING (MODERN PERSIAN/FARSI)
The optimal pathway to learn the Persian alphabet

PERSIAN SCRIPT HACKING (MODERN PERSIAN/FARSI)
The optimal pathway to learn the Persian alphabet

Developed with an algorithm that guarantees the most efficient route to success

Judith Meyer

British Library Cataloguing in Publication Data: a catalogue record for this title is available from the British Library.

Library of Congress Catalog Card Number: on file.

978 1 473 68002 9

1

Typeset by Integra Software Services Pvt., Pondicherry, India.

Printed and bound in Great Britain by Clays Ltd, Elcograf S.p.A.

John Murray Press policy is to use papers that are natural, renewable and recyclable products and made from wood grown in sustainable forests. The logging and manufacturing processes are expected to conform to the environmental regulations of the country of origin.

Carmelite House
50 Victoria Embankment
London EC4Y 0DZ

www.hodder.co.uk

CONTENTS

Dedicated to Chuck, who gave me invaluable support
throughout the process of writing this series.

A NOTE FROM JUDITH

Despite having learnt a number of languages to an advanced level, I often had great difficulty memorizing things. I always looked for shortcuts, tips, tricks and techniques to make learning that little bit easier. Some of this was probably overkill, but when it comes to my method for learning scripts however, I am convinced that I hit gold.

Letters are introduced one at a time alongside a lot of fun, puzzle-based reading practice, which helps you to learn the new letter effortlessly, and to review those you already know at the same time. Unlike other courses, which often provide a list of all letters of a new alphabet and encourage you to learn them ahead of the first lesson, *Persian Script Hacking* focuses solely on the letters themselves, so you can use it as a foundation for future study or for a fast, effective overview of the basics.

I don't go into Persian grammar – there are other courses for that – or even word usage. I ignore controversies. I also don't claim to be an expert about the Persian language (just an expert on learning writing systems) – that's why I worked with native speakers and a wonderful teacher of Persian; without them, this course would not have been possible.

My gratitude goes to Emma Green, who saw this method and believed in it enough to convince John Murray Learning to publish it within the Teach Yourself series, to Shabnam-Mir Afzali (Senior Fellow in Persian at SOAS, University of London) for native-speaker advice, and to DiEM25, my employer, who gave me enough space and support to write this book alongside my work for them.

Judith Meyer

INTRODUCTION TO THE SCRIPT AND TRANSLITERATION

The Persian script, as used in Modern Persian, or Farsi, is used by over 100 million Persian speakers worldwide, mainly in Iran and neighbouring countries. It is a variation of the Arabic alphabet.

There are two major differences from the Latin alphabet (the alphabet used to write English). The first difference is that Persian is written and read from right to left. This means that when you see a line like

AN

A is the first letter and **N** is the second; the line reads **AN**. In order to copy the line, you would start at the right edge of your page, start drawing from the tip of the straight line at the right (the Persian letter **A**), move down, then draw the curve of the next letter (the Persian letter **N**) starting from the top right going to the top left, and finally place the dot on top.

The second difference is that Persian is a cursive script; almost all letters are connected to each other, even in print. This means that, although you do not have to learn a whole new way of writing the letters to be able to decipher handwriting, you do have to learn to recognize each letter in its connected shapes straight away. Whenever this course introduces a new letter, you will see four forms: one showing the letter as it occurs in isolation (isolated), one as it is at the end of a word (final), one as it is in the middle of a word (medial), and one as it is at the beginning of a word (initial). Here are the shapes of the Persian letter **Be**:

isolated	final	medial	initial

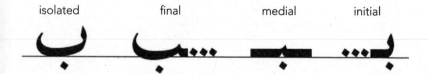

This means that if you use the letter **B** in isolation, it would simply be ب. If you want to write **ba** however, you have to use the initial form of it and then mesh it with the letter **A** (which is a vertical line in Persian), so it becomes با And here's how to write the non-existent word **bbb**, connecting three **B**s together so that you can see all their shapes:

Persian letters do not correspond exactly to English letters. There are several kinds of **S** for example, which do not sound different but have different shapes. In this course they will all be transliterated as **S**. This is in line with *Teach Yourself Complete Persian*, which you might use as a textbook after finishing this course, as well as the system used in Iran itself.

ALPHABET

The Persian alphabet consists of 32 letters. The letters are traditionally arranged by shape:

Persian letter	Transliteration	Name
ء	'	hamze
ا	ā	alef
ب	b	be
پ	p	pe
ت	t	te
ث	s	se
ج	j	je
چ	č	če
ح	h	he
خ	x	xe
د	d	dāl
ذ	z	zāl
ر	r	re
ز	z	ze
ژ	ž	že
س	s	sin
ش	š	šin
ص	s	sād
ض	z	zād
ط	t	tā

Persian letter	Transliteration	Name
ظ	z	zā
ع	´	´ayn
غ	q	qayn
ف	f	fe
ق	q	qaf
ک	k	kāf
گ	g	gāf
ل	l	lām
م	m	mim
ن	n	nun
و	v	vāv
ه	h	he
ی	y	ye

◁)) **01.01 Listen to the audio to hear how the letters are pronounced.**

LANGUAGE TIP

Look at the letters and notice how many of the letters look similar to the ones before or after, differing only by the number or position of dots.

You may be wondering about the lack of vowels. **Vāv** and **Ye** can be used to represent the long *OO* and *EE* sounds respectively. Short vowel sounds are not usually written down. Only the *Qur'an* and books for children or language learners contain written short vowels. These are diacritics, little markers above or below the other letters. In addition to the 32 letters, this course will also teach you those diacritics, from lesson 2 onwards, as well as a few special shapes (quasi-letters), so that you will have the tools to be able to read almost anything by the end.

HOW TO USE THIS COURSE

This course was created with the help of a cutting-edge computer algorithm that identified the optimal order to introduce the letters of the alphabet. Every section has been designed to build on top of the previous ones. Therefore it is important to study this course in a linear fashion rather than jumping back and forth.

Every lesson starts with a new letter. Look at it carefully and copy it down. There is space to copy the letters inside the book, but feel free to also copy the letters into an exercise book, especially if you are finding one of the letters more difficult to write than the others. You might even want to copy every Persian word in this course and later all the dialogues from your textbooks. Copying Persian will help you to get used to writing from right to left and also to improve your handwriting.

After copying the letter, you will be asked to find the letter in a short Persian text. This will increase your familiarity with it and will train your eyes to process Persian text as a series of letters rather than (as you may see it right now) a pretty drawing.

Next comes the core of the method: exercises where you have to read or write Persian words. These are real Persian words but they have been carefully chosen for their similarity to English. If you don't understand a word immediately, say it out loud or write down the transliteration and see if it sounds or looks familiar. The reason this method starts with such words is that it is much easier to learn the letters when you do not have to simultaneously learn new vocabulary. When children learn the alphabet at school, they also start by learning to read familiar words in their native language. Indeed, learning the alphabet is the foundation for learning everything else.

As you can see on the Alphabet pages, the transliteration (the way to render a Persian letter in the Latin alphabet, as used in English) is usually obvious, for example the Persian equivalent of the letter **M** is rendered as **M**, the Persian **N** is rendered as **N** and so on. Whenever it is not obvious, the lesson will tell you which Latin letter or letter combination has been chosen to render a given Persian letter.

Answers are provided in the Answer key at the end of this course, and you can listen to the sounds of the letters at library.teachyourself.com. Throughout the course, you will find #ScriptHacks to help you remember the letter and useful learning tips to help you to learn the language.

As mentioned previously, textbooks for language learners and children's books are printed with diacritics, markers above or below letters to indicate short vowels; adult native speakers are expected to be able to recognize the words and remember the non-printed vowels. This course begins with unvowelled Persian, and then introduces short vowels from the end of lesson two, so you can practise reading words with the short vowels in for the rest of the course, once you have been introduced to the first few letters.

Take as long as you need for this course. Some have completed it in a few hours; others have taken weeks, studying it more thoroughly and retaining more. The course has been divided into several 'lessons' with review sections to help you to find good places to stop for the day, but you can continue for as long as you want. In the end, what matters is that you become comfortable with the Persian script and that you have fun doing so! Good luck.

Icons

✏ Writing

📖 Reading

🔍 Spot the letter

◁)) Listening

 Script hack

1 FIRST LETTERS

Nun ن

As you may have guessed from the name, this is the Persian equivalent of the letter **N**.

As Persian is a cursive script, there are several possible shapes **Nun** can take:

#ScriptHack

To associate the picture and the sound, think of the curvy part as a boat, and the dot as the sun shining upon it at **N**oon.

Persian is read from right to left so the shape on the very right is how **Nun** will look at the beginning of a word (known as 'initial'); then the form when it is in the middle (known as 'medial'), and third from the right is the form it takes when at the end (known as 'final'). Finally, on the left is what **Nun** looks like when it is isolated, without other letters immediately before or after.

This is how to write the imaginary word **nnn**, using these different shapes:

ننن

🖊 **1 Practise writing Nun in its four distinct shapes.**

- -

#ScriptHack

When writing Persian by hand, move from right to left and write dots and diacritics last.

🔍 2 Find the six **Nuns** in the following paragraph.

برای یک سال دور دنیا سفر کردم.
از آسیا شروع کردم و بعد به آفریقا،
اروپا و آمریکا سفر کردم. در آسیا
کشورهای اندونزی، ویتنام، چین،
کره و ژاپن را خیلی دوست داشتم.

LANGUAGE TIP

There are several letters that have the same shape as **Nun**. The most reliable way to identify **Nun** is to look for the dot above, and then verify the shape.

Alef ا

Alef is the most commonly written vowel in Persian. You might be tempted to think that it is the equivalent of the English A, but that only occurs sometimes, at the beginning of words or in foreign loanwords – a sound

#ScriptHack

To remember the shape of **Alef**, think of it as being a stem down the centre of a leaf (**Alef**).

which is given the transliteration ā in most textbooks. Note also that **Alef** may appear with a tilde ~ on top when it is at the beginning of a word, but this does not change its pronunciation:

This is how to write the syllable **nā**, consisting of the letter **Nun** and the letter **Alef**:

Note how the **Alef** is connected to the end of the **Nun**. The same does not happen when writing **ān**, because **Alef** is special, in that, it only connects on one side:

Naan bread, which could be served at an Indian, Pakistani or Middle Eastern restaurant, originally comes from Persia. This is how to write it in Persian:

 #ScriptHack

Think of most Persian letters, including **Nun**, as pieces of double-sided tape which you join together. **Alef** and a few others, however, are like pieces of single-sided tape that can only join on one side.

✏ **3 Practise writing Alef.**

✏️ **4** Practise writing **naan**.

_____

- -

_____

📖 **5** Read the Persian letters and use the clues to work out the meaning of the following words.

🔊 **01.02**

a First name of singer Mouskouri:

نانا

b A common women's name:

آنا

Ye ی

This is **Ye**, the Persian equivalent of **Y**. The initial and medial forms look identical to those of **Nun**, except that there are two dots underneath rather than one on top. The final and isolated forms are different and do not have the dots.

 #ScriptHack

Ye's characteristic form looks like a water slide. As you trace it, imagine children going down the slide saying **Yay** and being happ**Y**.

Ye has two uses:

   1 as a consonant it's the same as the **Y** in _year_ (transliterated as **y**).

   2 as a vowel it sounds like the **Y** in _happy_, the same as the long **EE** in _me_ (transliterated as **i**).

6 Practise writing **Ye** in its four forms.

7 Find the twelve **Yes** in the following paragraph: nine in the initial or medial form and four in the final or isolated form.

برای یک سال دور دنیا سفر کردم.
از آسیا شروع کردم و بعد به آفریقا،
اروپا و آمریکا سفر کردم. در آسیا
کشورهای اندونزی، ویتنام، چین،
کره و ژاپن را خیلی دوست داشتم.

8 Read the Persian letters and use the clues to work out the meaning of the following words.

◁)) **01.03**

a A greeting:

ای

b Women's names:

آنی – نینا

Vāv و

This is **Vāv**, the Persian equivalent of **V** but also the last of the Persian vowel letters – it has a dual use just like **Ye**. When **Vāv** acts as a consonant, it is transliterated as **v**. When it acts as a vowel, it is transliterated **u** and pronounced as the **OO** in *boot*. Like **Alef**, **Vāv** only connects to the preceding letter:

🖊 **9** Practise writing **Vāv** in its two forms.

🔍 **10** Find the five **Vāv**s in the following paragraph.

برای یک سال دور دنیا سفر کردم.
از آسیا شروع کردم و بعد به آفریقا،
اروپا و آمریکا سفر کردم.

LANGUAGE TIP

Vāv is also used to represent **W** in foreign names, and in Afghanistan **Vāv** is actually pronounced as **w** rather than **v**.

📖 **11** Read the Persian letters and use the clues to work out the meaning of the following words.

🔊) **01.04**

a Russian name: ايوان

b English name: وينى

c Chinese currency: يوان

d American state: آيووا

✏️ **12** Copy the names you have just read.

Te ت

This is **Te**, the Persian equivalent of **T**. It looks similar to **Nun**, but with two dots. Note that the curve of the final and isolated forms does not dip nearly as deep as for **Nun**. There are several more letters that follow the **Te** scheme, which you will learn later.

#ScriptHack

Try to imagine **Te** as a tent.

ت ـت ـتـ تـ ت

✏️ **13** Practise writing **Te** in its four forms.

🔍 **14** Find the three Tes in the following paragraph.

در آسیا کشورهای اندونزی،
ویتنام، چین، کره و ژاپن را خیلی
دوست داشتم.

📖 **15** Read the Persian letters and use the clues to work out the meaning of the following words.

🔊 **01.05**

ویتنی – آنتونیو

a Names:

یوتا – تایوان

b Geography:

ات

c Key on your keyboard:

✏️ **16** Copy the Persian words you have just read.

REVIEW

Here are all the letters you have learnt so far:

ن	و	ی	ت	ا

✏️ **1** Copy the Persian letters and give their letter names too.

📖 **2** Do you recognize this name?

تونی

📖 **3** Here are some useful Persian words that are different from English. Write down their transliteration.

Persian	Transliteration	Meaning
تو	_____	*you*
آن	_____	*that*
تا	_____	*until*

✏️ **4** Practise writing the letters you have learnt in this section.

2 LINES AND CIRCLES

Lām ل

This is the Persian equivalent of the English letter **L**.

#ScriptHack

Lām looks like a mirrored **L**.

🖉 **1** Practise writing **Lām** in its four forms.

🔍 **2** Find the four **Lāms** in the following paragraph.

قاهره خیلی شلوغ بود و صحرا
بسیار گرم. اما رودخانه نیل و
اهرام ثلاثه واقعاً زیبا بودند.

LANGUAGE TIP

If unsure whether something is a **Lām** or **Alef**, note the following: in final or isolated position, they can be distinguished because **Lām** has a tail, and in initial and medial position **Alef** does not exist (it cannot connect to the following letter, hence **Alef** is always final or isolated).

📖 **3** Read the Persian letters and use the clues to work out the meaning of the following words.

🔊 **02.01**

a Greeting on the phone:

b Countries:

c Cities:

d River in Africa:

e Name:

الو

ايتاليا – ليتوانى

تالين – ليون

نيل

لوتى

LANGUAGE TIP

When a word starts with **Alef-Ye**, the **Alef** is silent, i.e. the word starts with the vowel **I**.

 #ScriptHack

In order to quickly distinguish Arabic text from Persian, look for the very characteristic الـ (**al...**) which is the Arabic word for *the*. In Arabic texts it is used all the time, in Persian you find it very rarely.

Mim م

Mim is the Persian equivalent of the letter **M**.

The pronunciation of this letter is really simple: it is the same as the English letter **M**, as in *mouse*. Most Persian letters are formed in a clockwise fashion, but **Mim** is an exception as it is anti-clockwise, at least in the initial format.

 #ScriptHack

To remember this letter, imagine it looking like a **M**ouse, and when it's hanging you can see the tail.

4 Practise writing **Mim** in its initial form. Start at the bottom left of the circle and move anti-clockwise.

5 Practise writing **Mim** in its medial form. Start on the right (where the previous letter ended), draw the circle clockwise and then place your pen to the left of it.

6 Practise writing **Mim** in its final form. Follow the same pattern as for the medial form, but end with a tail.

✏️ **7** Practise writing **Mim** in its isolated form. Start at the top, draw a
kind of half circle and then go straight down.

مـ

🔍 **8** Find the seven **Mims** in the following paragraph.

در آسیا کشورهای اندونزی، ویتنام، چین،
کره و ژاپن را خیلی دوست داشتم.
سوشی و چای ژاپنی خیلی خوشمزه بود!
در آفریقا، اتیوپی، موزامبیک و مصر را
خیلی دوست داشتم.

📖 **9** Read the Persian letters and use the clues to work out the meaning
of the following words.

🔊 **02.02**

a Names:

تیم – تام – ویلیام

b Countries:

مالت – مالی

c Cities: لیما – مانیل

d Chemical elements: آلومینیوم – لیتیوم – تیتانیوم

e Words borrowed from English: میلیون – ویتامین

Zir

Persian short vowels (all except **Alef**, **Ye** and **Vāv**) are indicated through diacritics, i.e. small lines that are written above or below the consonant that comes before

#ScriptHack

All dots and diacritics are normally written last.

them. The Persian short **E** sound, as in the name *Ben*, is indicated by a small diagonal line underneath the preceding consonant. The Persian name of this diacritic is **Zir**. This is the name *Ben* in Persian:

بِن

This is the name *Emma* – remember that when another vowel is present, the initial **Alef** is silent; it is only needed as a carrier:

اِما

LANGUAGE TIP

Persian, like Arabic, does not produce much text with diacritics. Only textbooks for language learners and children's books are printed with them; adult native speakers are expected to be able to recognize the words and remember the non-printed vowels. Therefore, try not to rely on them too much.

✏️ **10** Copy the two Persian words with **Zir** from above.

_____

- -

_____

📖 **11** Read the Persian letters and use the clues to work out the meaning of the following words.

🔊 **02.03**

a Female names:

اِوا – لِنا

b Male names:

ايتِن – آلِن – نيتِن

c Asian currency:

يِن

d Asian country:

ويِتنام

e European cities:

آتِن – نانت

f Russian leader:

لِنين

LANGUAGE TIP

When dealing with unvowelled Persian texts (those lacking **Zir** and other diacritics), you'll have to guess whether **Vāv** is pronounced **V** or **U** and whether **Ye** is pronounced **Y** or **I**. In vowelled texts however, you can tell by seeing whether the previous letter is a vowel. After a vowel, the next letter should be a consonant, not another vowel. And after a consonant, for ease of pronunciation the next letter should be a vowel, not a **V** or **Y**.

Re ر

Re is the equivalent of the letter **R** in
English, but it does not sound much
like the English **R**, rather like the
Spanish **R**. You may have heard it when
a Spanish (or Italian) speaker calls for *María*.

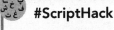

#ScriptHack

To remember this letter, you
might think that **Re** looks like a
lower-case **r**, but upside down.

The shape is similar to **Vāv**, but without the loop:

Re is another one-sided letter that does not attach itself to anything after it.

ر ـر

✏️ **12 Practise writing Re in its two forms.**

🔍 **13 Find the eleven Res in the following paragraph.**

برای یک سال دور دنیا سفر کردم.
از آسیا شروع کردم و بعد به آفریقا،
اروپا و آمریکا سفر کردم.

14 Read the Persian letters and use the clues to work out the meaning of the following words.

🔊 **02.04**

a Three variations on the same name: — ماری – ماریا
مِری

b More names: تِری – روت

c Famous woman: مِریلین مونرو

d Indispensable: اینتِرنِت

e Cities: – تورِنتو – تیرانا – تورین
مونترِآل

f Countries: ایران – موریتانی – رومانی

Be ب

Be, the Persian equivalent of the letter **B**, has exactly the same shapes as **Te**, except that it has one dot below rather than two dots above the line.

#ScriptHack

Think of **Be** as representing a **B**oat.

ب ــبـ ــب ب

✏️ **15** Practise writing **Be** in its four forms.

🔍 **16** Find the five **Bes** in the following paragraph.

در آفریقا، اتیوپی، موزامبیک و مصر را خیلی دوست داشتم. قاهره خیلی شلوغ بود و صحرا بسیار گرم. اما رودخانه نیل و اهرام ثلاثه واقعاً زیبا بودند.

📖 **17** Read the Persian letters and use the clues to work out the meaning of the following words.

🔊 **02.05**

a Rod:

بار

b Names:

باربارا – بنیامین – بنی – بتی – بیل – برایان – رابرت

c Cities: ملبورن – برلین – بالتیمور – بولونیا – بیروت – نایروبی

d Countries: بریتانیا – آلبانی – بِنین – نامیبیا

e Famous singer: باب مارلی

✎ **18** Copy the names from 17b.

REVIEW

You have come a long way! Here are all the letters you have learnt so far, excluding diacritics:

م ل ر ن و ی ت ب ا

✏ **1** Copy the Persian letters and give their letter names too.

📖 **2** Your Iranian friend is hosting a party and has made a list of friends to invite. Read the list and say the names out loud.

ویلیام   بیلی   بارون

روت   بِن   تِری

لِنا   ماریا

✏ **3** Add the following names of people to the list: *Terry, Alan, Benjamin*.

3 LETTERS LIKE WAVES

Kāf ک

This is the Persian equivalent of the letter **K**.

ک ـک ـک ک

#ScriptHack

Kāf looks like the right side of **K** in its initial and medial forms.

✏ **1** Practise writing **Kāf** in its four forms.

🔍 **2** Find the five **Kāf**s in the following paragraph.

برای یک سال دور دنیا سفر کردم.
از آسیا شروع کردم و بعد به آفریقا،
اروپا و آمریکا سفر کردم.

📖 **3** Read the Persian letters and use the clues to work out the meaning
of the following words.

🔊 **03.01**

a Names: کاترین – کارمِن – مونیکا – مایک – مایکِل

b Countries: کِنیا – کوبا – کامِرون – موناکو – اوکراین

c Cities: توکیو – بانکوک – کیتو – کانبِرا – نیویورک – آنکارا

d Food and drink: کاری – کیوی – موکا

e Former US presidents: بیل کِلینتون – باراک اوباما

f Famous writers: تالکین – مارک تواین

g Words borrowed from English:

نیکِل – باکتِری – کاریکاتور
– اِلِکتِرونیکی – کیلومِتر

4 Write the following names in Persian, using only the letters you already know: *Mark*, *Kim*, *Kevin*.

Sin س

Sin is one of the ways to write **S** in Persian.

In the final and isolated positions, **Sin** has the same kind of arc as **Nun**, but its main characteristics are the three bumps at the beginning.

#ScriptHack

To remember **Sin**, picture the three bumps which look like the waves of the **S**ea. When you see sea waves, think **S**.

✏ **5** Practise writing **Sin** in its four forms.

🔍 **6** Find the five **Sins** in the following paragraph.

چیزهای زیادی درباره تولستوی،
شکسپیر، گوته، شیلر و کارل مارکس
یادگرفتم. به موسیقی موتزارت،
باخ و چایکوفسکی گوش کردم.

LANGUAGE TIP

Words beginning with **S** followed by another consonant are not common in Persian. You will usually find a short **E** has been inserted at the beginning of the word, which allows the consonant cluster to be broken up, e.g. Persian speakers wouldn't say *Ski* but *Es-ki* (اِسکی).

📖 **7** Read the Persian letters and use the clues to work out the meaning of the following words.

🔊 **03.02**

a Sports: تِنیس – بِیسبال – بوکس

b Music styles: اِسکا – سالسا

c Names: بوریس – اِستیوِن

d Famous writers: کیتس – سارتِر – تولستوی

e European cities: لیسبون – اِستانبول – بارسِلون – بِریستول – نیوکاسِل – والِنسیا

f Parts of the world: سیبِری – آسام – آسیا

✏️ **8** Write the following words in Persian, using only the letters you already know: *samba*, *taxi* (**taksi**), *virus*.

Dāl د

This is the Persian equivalent of the letter **D**.

Like **Vāv** and **Alef**, **Dāl** is also one-sided, meaning that it attaches itself to the previous letter but does not allow any following letter to attach to it. Hence there are only two forms:

#ScriptHack

The isolated form of **Dāl** has the curve of a **D**, and the other form is just short of a mirrored **D**.

د ـد

✏ **9** Practise writing **Dāl** in its two forms.

🔍 **10** Find the ten **Dāl**s in the following paragraph.

برای یک سال دور دنیا سفر کردم.
از آسیا شروع کردم و بعد به آفریقا،
اروپا و آمریکا سفر کردم. در آسیا
کشورهای اندونزی، ویتنام، چین،
کره و ژاپن را خیلی دوست داشتم.

📖 **11** Read the Persian letters and use the clues to work out the meaning of the following words.

🔊 **03.03**

a Countries: کانادا – برمودا – سودان – دانمارک – آندورا – رواندا – اکوادور

b Cities: سیدنی – مادرید – آمستِردام – دوبلین – روتِردام

c Names: الکساندر – سیندی – دَیمیتری – اِدی – اِدوارد

d Famous singers: سِلین دیون – باب دیلِن

e Types of movies: ایندی – دِرام

✏️ **12** Write the following words in Persian, using only the letters you already know: *radio*, *lemonade* (**limunād**), *democrat*.

Piš

Piš is a diacritic, like **Zir**. It is a small bow above the letter and stands for a short /o/ sound, like the **o** in *hotel*. When foreign names involve a long **O**, they use **Vāv** rather than **Piš** in Persian.

The name of the Sri Lankan capital Colombo is spelt with two **Piš** and one **Vāv** in Persian:

When a word starts with a short **O**, the **Piš** is placed on top of **Alef**. As diacritics like **Piš** are not typically included in texts for native speakers, this means that you may sometimes see an **Alef** in unvowelled text that is pronounced as /o/ – or like /e/ if it carries an unwritten **Zir**. This only occurs at the beginning of words because elsewhere the **Piš** and the **Zir** can be placed on the preceding consonant.

This is the name of the country Jordan in Persian, with **Piš** on **Alef**:

اُردُن

✏ **13** Copy the Persian spelling of *Colombo* and *Jordan* from above. Write them several times until writing the **Piš** feels comfortable.

📖 **14** Read the Persian letters and use the clues to work out the meaning of the following words.

🔊 **03.04**

a Names:

دُن – اُدین – اُدری – بُروس – اُسکار – اُتو

b Cities:

اُسلو – رُم – مُسکو – اُتاوا – کابُل – اُمسک

c Countries:

اُسترالیا – کُلمبیا – بوتسُوانا – سامُوآ

d Chemical elements:

سُدیُم – کُبالت – بُرُم – یُد – اورانیُم

e International word:

اُتوبوس

✏️ **15** Write the following words in Persian, using only the letters you already know: *doctor, comedy.*

Gāf گ

Gāf is the Persian equivalent of the letter **G**.

گ گ ـگ ـگ

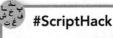

#ScriptHack

Remember **Kāf**? **Gāf** is a modified version of **Kāf**, just as **K** and **G** are very similar in sound.

✏ **16** Practise writing **Gāf** in its four forms.

🔍 **17** Find the four **Gāf**s in the following paragraph.

نقاشی های سالوادور دالی و وینسنت ون گوگ را دیدم. چیزهای زیادی درباره تولستوی، شکسپیر، گوته، شیلر و کارل مارکس یادگرفتم.

Read the Persian letters and use the clues to work out the meaning of the following words.

🔊 03.05

a Russian names: اُلگا – اُلِگ – یِوگِنی

b Countries: کُنگو – اوگاندا – ماداگاسکار – سِنگال

c What to call England in Persian: اِنگِلِستان

d Cities: کینگستون – بِلگَراد – اِدینبورگ – رِیگا – وِلینگتون – سانتیاگو

e Inspiring leaders: گوتاما بودا – مارتین لوتِر کینگ – گاندی

f International words: بولینگ – گیتار – یوگا – رِگی

REVIEW

Here are all the letters you have learnt so far, not including diacritics:

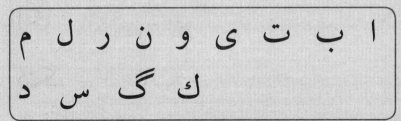

م ل ر ن و ی ت ب ا

د س گ ک

✏ **1** Copy the Persian letters and give their letter names too.

📖 **2** This manhole cover says *water*. What is the word in Persian?

✏ **3** You are planning a tour of some cities in Iran. Note down the city names in Persian: **Arāk, Kermān, Sāri, Gorgān**.

4 DOTS AND DIACRITICS

Pe پ

This is the Persian equivalent of the English letter **P**. Arabic does not have this letter, it only has **Be**, so Persian

#ScriptHack

Pe looks like a **P**addleboat.

took the letter **Be** ب and added two extra dots underneath in order to create **Pe** پ. The forms are otherwise identical.

✏ **1** Practise writing **Pe** in its four forms.

🔍 **2** Find the three **Pes** in the following paragraph.

در آسیا کشورهای اندونزی، ویتنام، چین، کره و ژاپن را خیلی دوست داشتم. سوشی و چای ژاپنی خیلی

خوشمزه بود! در آفریقا، اتیوپی، موزامبیک و مصر را خیلی دوست داشتم.

📖 **3** Read the Persian letters and use the clues to work out the meaning of the following words.

◁)) **04.01**

a Foods:

پاستا – پاپایا

b Countries:

پاکِستان – پرو – نِپال – پانآما – اسپاَنیا

c European cities:

پاریس – پراگ – بوداپِست – پورتو – آنتِورپ – لیوِرپول

d North American cities:

مینیاپولیس – تِمپا – پیتسبِرگ –
ایندیاناپُلیس – وینیپِگ

e Great astronomers:

کوپِرنیک – کِپلِر

f Planets:

نِپتون – پُلوتون

g International words:

پارک – اُپِرا –
دیپلُماسی

🖉 **4** Write the following names in Persian based on how they are pronounced, not how they are spelt in English: *Paul, Peter, Pierre*.

Zebar

Zebar, like **Zir** and **Piš**, is a short vowel that is indicated as a diacritic rather than a full letter. **Zebar** takes the form of a short line above the consonant and the sound it produces is **a** as in *hat*. This is different from the long **ā** of **Alef**. **Zebar** can also be placed on top of **Alef** at the beginning of a word to indicate that the word starts with this sound rather than **ā**.

·**Zebar** completes your set of Persian vowels: **Alef** (ā), **Yaa** (i) and **Vāv** (u), and the diacritics **Zebar** (a), **Zir** (e) and **Piš** (o).

This is how to spell Miami in Persian: مَیامی

Note that the Persian pronunciation differs from ours. They call the city

mayāmi. And this is Madras: مَدرَس

✏ **5** Copy the Persian spelling of *Miami* and *Madras* from above. Write them several times until writing the **Zebar** feels comfortable.

> _____
>
> _____
>
> _____
>
> _____

📖 **6** Read the Persian letters and use the clues to work out the meaning of the following words.

◁)) **04.02**

a Names:

آدَم – آدرِیَن – اَگنِس –

پَت – مَت

b English-speaking cities:

لَندَن – آوکلَند

وَنکوور – پورتلَند – کَلگَری –

کِلیولَند – اَبِردین – بیرمَنگام

c Countries:

تایلَند – ایرلَند – یَمَن –
سَنگاپور – ایسلَند –
تُرکَمَنِستان

d International words:

رَپ – اَلکُل – اَتُم –
کیلوگِرَم – تَنباکو

✏ **7** How would Persian speakers spell the names of *Batman* and *Superman*? Hint: they do not use **Alef**.

He ه

He is one of the two ways to write **H** in Persian. It also has a special role: in Persian, no word may end in one of the diacritics (**Zebar**, **Piš** and **Zir**). However, a lot of Persian words end in **E**. Persian therefore uses **He** to indicate a final **E**.

> **#ScriptHack**
>
> With the eye-like initial shape and the fly-like medial shape, this letter is very memorable.

This also has the advantage that this sound becomes more visible, because the diacritics are often unwritten while **He** is always written.

ه ـه ـهـ هـ

🖉 **8** Practise writing **He** in its initial form. Start at the top of the circle and move clockwise until you have almost completed an oval, then draw a smaller arc inside the first, and move out.

🖉 **9** Practise writing **He** in its medial form. Start at the right (where the previous letter ended), then draw the upper circle clockwise and then the lower circle counterclockwise, just as you draw the number. Finish on the main line again and move to the left.

🖉 **10** Practise writing **He** in its final form. First draw the semistraight line up, then add the nose.

🖊 **11** Practise writing **He** in its isolated form, starting at the top and then draw a circle clockwise.

ه

🔍 **12** Find the four **Hes** in the following paragraph.

چیزهای زیادی درباره تولستوی،
شکسپیر، گوته، شیلر و کارل مارکس
یادگرفتم. به موسیقی موتزارت،
باخ و چایکوفسکی گوش کردم.

📖 **13** Read the Persian letters and use the clues to work out the meaning of the following words.

🔊 **04.03**

a Exclamations:

ها ها – آها

b Magicians, or wizards:

هودینی – هَری پاتِر

c Countries: روسیه – تُرکیه – سوریه –
هُلَند – هُندوراس

d Places for holidays: باهاما – هاوایی

e Asian cities: هُنگ کُنگ – تایپه –
دهلی نو – هانوی
آگَره

f Northern European cities:

هِلسینکی – کُپنهاگ –
هَامبورگ – استِکهُلم

g Names: هانا – هِلِن

14 Write the following words in Persian, using only the letters you already know: *hotel*, *congress* (called **kongere** in Persian), *hamburger*, *minaret* (**mināre**), *karate*.

Ze ز

For historic reasons, Persian has several ways to write the **Z** sound. **Ze** is one of them. **Ze** looks exactly like **Re** with an extra dot on top. It is also one-sided, like **Re**.

> **#ScriptHack**
>
> To remember that this letter sounds like **Z**, imagine it as a dolphin balancing a ball on its nose at a **Z**oo.

Hence there are only two forms:

ز — ـز

15 Practise writing Ze in its two forms.

🔍 **16** Find the three **Zes** in the following paragraph.

در آسیا کشورهای اندونزی، ویتنام،
چین، کره و ژاپن را خیلی دوست
داشتم. سوشی و چای ژاپنی خیلی
خوشمزه بود! در آفریقا، اتیوپی،
موزامبیک و مصر را خیلی دوست
داشتم.

📖 **17** Read the Persian letters and use the clues to work out the meaning
of the following words.

🔊 **04.04**

a Countries:

بِرِزیل – نیوزیلَند –
اَندونِزی – اُزبَکستان –
زیمبابوه – موزامبیک

b Cities: مِکزیکو سیتی – زاگِرب –
بازِل – بِریزبِن –
سَن پِترزبورگ

c Things you will find on a map of Britain: لیدز – وِلز –
تِیمز

d They greatly influenced our culture: بیتِلز –
والت دیزنی

e International words: پیتزا – بازار – دیزِل –
سوسیالیزم – تِلِویزیون

🖉 **18** Write the following names in Persian, using **Ze** whenever you hear the **Z** sound as in *zoo*: Suzy, Susan, Liza, Zachary, Elizabeth.

Jim ج

Jim is the Persian equivalent of the
letter **J** as in *jungle*.

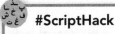

#ScriptHack

To remember the shape of **Jim**,
think of it as an open **J**aw.

✎ **19** Practise writing **Jim** in its four forms.

🔍 **20** Find the three **Jims** in the following paragraph.

به موسیقی موتزارت، باخ و
چایکوفسکی گوش کردم. در آمریکا
با دوستم، مارک از یک ساحل به
ساحل دیگر سفر کردیم. از ایالات
بسیاری دیدار کردیم. مثل
نیویورک، نیو همشایر، ماساچوست،

ویرجینیا، نیوجرزی و اوکلاهوما.
تکیلا و ویسکی نوشیدیم و دوستان
جدید پیدا کردیم.

LANGUAGE TIP

Some English words and names that use this sound are also spelt with a
G, for example the word *giant*.

📖 **21** Read the Persian letters and use the clues to work out the meaning
of the following words.

🔊 **04.05**

a Names:

جینا – اَنجی – جُرج –
جَک – جیمز – جِنی –
جودی – جولیا

b Cities:

جاکارتا – لُس آنجِلِس –
نانجینگ

c Countries:

نیجِریه – کامبوج –
تاجیکِستان – جیبوتی

d US states:

جورجیا – نیوجِرسی –
ویرجینیا

e Famous musicians:

جیمی هِندریکس –
میک جَگِر
جان لِنون

22 Write the following words in Persian, using only letters you already know: *jazz, judo, ninja, jeans* (**jin**).

REVIEW

Here are all the letters you have learnt so far, except the diacritics:

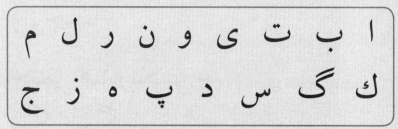

🖊 **1** Copy the Persian letters and give their letter names too.

📖 **2** You are looking to buy tea in an Iranian supermarket. You find a pack that says 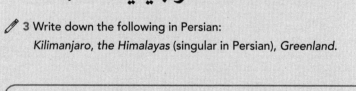 on it. What is it?

🖊 **3** Write down the following in Persian:
   Kilimanjaro, *the Himalayas* (singular in Persian), *Greenland*.

5 FEATHERS

Fe ف

Fe, the Persian **F**, has one dot on top like **Nun**, but the shape is very different.

#ScriptHack

To help you to remember it, think of the loopy part of **Fe** as the representation of a **Feather**.

🖉 **1** Practise writing **Fe** in its four forms.

🔍 **2** Find the three Fes in the following paragraph.

برای یک سال دور دنیا سفر کردم.
از آسیا شروع کردم و بعد به آفریقا،
اروپا و آمریکا سفر کردم.

📖 3 Read the Persian letters and use the clues to work out the meaning of the following words.

🔊 05.01

a Cities and towns in the UK: کاردیف – بلفاست –
آکسفورد – هَلیفَکس

b Countries and US states: کالیفُرنیا – فِلوریدا –
فیلیپین – فَرانسه –
فیجی

c More cities: سان فِرانسیسکو –
دوسلدورف –
فِرانکفورت – هانوفِر

d Famous Germans: زیگموند فِروید –
کافکا

e What internet addicts cannot do without: وایفای

4 Write the following words in Persian using the letters you already know: *film, golf, telephone.*

Hamze ء

The **Hamze** is a diacritic. The **hamze** in Persian does not usually sit by itself. Like Arabic – where it has come from – it can sit on an **Alef** as well as on a '**vav**' ؤ or on a plate. It is pronounced as a glottal stop – like the sound in between 'uh-oh'. If you do not hear any sound there, compare saying 'uh, oh' and 'uh-oh'. The difference is the glottal stop. The glottal stop is marked with a **Hamze** in Persian script. In transliteration it becomes an apostrophe.

This is the name of Nicaragua's capital, Managua, in Persian:

ماناگوئه

Therefore it is pronounced **Mānāgu-e**. Without the **Hamze**, one would think that **Vāv** is a consonant here and pronounce it **Mānāgve**. **Hamze** primarily occurs when there are two vowels in a row.

5 Copy the name *Managua* from above several times.

📖 **6** Read the Persian letters and use the clues to work out the meaning of the following words.

🔊 **05.02**

a Countries:

هائیتی – اِسرائیل –
پاراگوئه – جامائیکا

b Cities:

بوئنوس آیرس – سائوپائولو –
ماکائو – نیواورلِئان

c Names:

نائومی – مَنوئِل – پائولو –
لِئوناردو

d International words:

نِئون – تِئاتر – ویدئو

✏️ **7** Write the following names in Persian using the letters you already know: *Napoleon, Cleopatra.*

Šin ش

Šin is pronounced as the **sh** in *fish*. In terms of writing, all its forms are identical to those of **Sin**, just with three extra dots on top. The dots can become a ^ shape in handwriting.

ش ـش ـشـ شـ

✏ **8** Practise writing **Š**in in its four forms.

🔍 **9** Find the four **Š**ins in the following paragraph.

مثل نیویورک، نیو همشایر،
ماساچوست، ویرجینیا، نیوجرزی و
اوکلاهوما. تکیلا و ویسکی
نوشیدیم و دوستان جدید پیدا
کردیم. خیلی خوش گذشت.

10 Read the Persian letters and use the clues to work out the meaning of the following words.

05.03

a Names:

ناتاشا – پاتریشیا – ماشا

b Cities:

واشینگتُن – شانگهای – شیکاگو – اِشتوتگارت – نَشویل

c Great writers:

شِکسپیر – شیلِر – پوشکین

d International words:

ماشین – ریکشا – شاه – سوشی

11 The following country names differ somewhat in Persian and English. Write them in Persian based on the given transliteration: *Chile* (**šile**), *Austria* (**otriš**), *Morocco* (**marākeš**).

Če چ

Če is a letter that doesn't exist in Arabic. It is pronounced as the **CH** in *check*. Če looks exactly like **Jim**, but with three dots instead of one.

#ScriptHack

Since we associated **Jim** with a jaw, think of Če's extra dots as teeth ready to cat**CH** something.

🖋 **12** Practise writing Če in its four forms.

🔍 **13** Find the two Čes in the following paragraph.

در آسیا کشورهای اندونزی، ویتنام، چین، کره و ژاپن را خیلی دوست داشتم. سوشی و چای ژاپنی خیلی خوشمزه بود!

📖 **14** Read the Persian letters and use the clues to work out the meaning of the following words.

🔊 **05.04**

a Names:

چارلز – ریچارد

b Cities and towns: مَنچِستِر – ریچموند – راچِستِر – چنگدو – چِنای – کَراچی

c Countries and US states: ماساچوسِت – چاد – چِک – چین

d Great artists: لِئوناردو دا وینچی – چایکوفسکی

e British Prime Minister: وینستون چِرچیل

f Native American peoples: چِروکی – آپاچی

✏️ **15** Write the following words in Persian using the letters you already know: *chai, tai chi, lychee.*

Qaf ق

Qaf is a sound that doesn't exist in English. You have probably heard it at some point though, because it is the sound of the Dutch **G** / Russian **Ge** / Greek **Gamma**. It is a vibrating sound articulated in the same place as the English **G**. Be sure to listen to the recordings.

#ScriptHack

As we associated the shapes of **Fe** with a **Feather**, **Qaf** could be a particularly big feather.

The forms of **Qaf** look like **Fe** with two dots instead of one. However, note that **Fe**'s tail never goes below the line, while **Qaf**'s tail does in its final and isolated forms.

✏ **16** Practise writing **Qaf**.

🔍 **17** Find the three Qafs in the following paragraph.

در آفریقا، اتیوپی، موزامبیک و مصر را
خیلی دوست داشتم. قاهره خیلی شلوغ
بود و صحرا بسیار گرم. اما رودخانه
نیل و اهرام ثلاثه واقعا زیبا بودند.

📖 **18** Read the Persian letters and use the clues to work out the meaning of the following words.

🔊 **05.05**

a Muslim holy book:

قُرآن

b Continent:

آفریقا

c Countries:

مَقدونیه – قَزاقِستان – قِرقیزِستان

d Something to listen to:

موسیقی

✏️ **19** The word *coffee* in English derives from the Arabic **qahwe**, still the word for *coffee* in Persian today. Write it in Persian letters.

REVIEW

Here are all the letters you have learnt so far, except for diacritics:

ا ب ت ی و ن ر ل م

ك گ س د پ ه ز ج ف

ء ش چ ق

✏ **1 Copy the Persian letters and give their letter names too.**

📖 **2** Compare the Persian spelling of these city names to their English names.

🖊 **3** Copy the Persian city names from the picture and add any missing vowel diacritics.

6 JAWS

Že ژ

This letter is pronounced like the **S** in *pleasure*. It is a softer sound than the **J** of **Jim**. It is another non-connecting letter, with letter shapes identical to those of **Re** and **Ze**, except with three dots.

#ScriptHack

The three dots on **Že**, which are the only difference between **Že** ژ and **Ze** ز, are the equivalent of the hat that distinguishes the letter **Ž** from **Z**.

✏️ **1** Practise writing **Že** in its two forms.

🔍 **2** Find the two **Žes** in the following paragraph.

در آسیا کشورهای اندونزی، ویتنام، چین، کره و ژاپن را خیلی دوست داشتم. سوشی و چای ژاپنی خیلی خوشمزه بود!

📖 **3** Read the Persian letters and use the clues to work out the meaning of the following words.

🔊 **06.01**

a Countries: ژاپُن – آرژانتین

b Cities: ژوهانِسبورگ – ژِنو – ریو دو ژانیرو – شِنژِن

c Ruler of an ancient empire: ژولیوس سِزار

d Chemical elements: نیتروژِن – هیدروژِن اُکسیژِن

e Place for a car: گاراژ

f Kind of drama: تِراژِدی

LANGUAGE TIP

Not many languages have the letter **Ž**. Instead you may find this sound spelt as **ZH**, **J** or **G**. Some, mainly older, Persian textbooks will spell it as **ZH** for ease of printing.

4 The Persian names of Belgium and Norway are derived from the French pronunciation of these country names: **Belgique (belžik)** and **Norvège (norvež)**. Write these down in Persian letters.

Xe خ

This letter is pronounced like the Spanish **X** in the name *Xavier*, the German **CH** in *Bach*, or the Scottish **CH** in *loch*. The shape is exactly like **Jim**, but the dot is on top rather than underneath/inside.

#ScriptHack

Jim was associated with a jaw. **Xe** also looks like a jaw, but this is Xavier's jaw and Xavier has a mole in his face.

خ ـخ ـخـ خـ

5 Practise writing **Xe** in its four forms.

🔍 **6** Find the four Xes in the following paragraph.

در آسیا کشورهای اندونزی، ویتنام، چین، کره و ژاپن را خیلی دوست داشتم. سوشی و چای ژاپنی خیلی خوشمزه بود! در آفریقا، اتیوپی، موزامبیک و مصر را خیلی دوست داشتم.

📖 **7** Read the Persian letters and use the clues to work out the meaning of the following words.

🔊 **06.02**

a Common Arabic name:

خالِد

b Cities:

زوریخ – بُخارِست –
مونیخ – اوترِخت –
سان خوزه – سَن خوآن

c Great composer:

$$باخ$$

d Great writer:

$$چِخوف$$

📖 **8** The English words *caliph* (for a Muslim ruler) and *caliphate* are derived from the Arabo-Persian word **xalife**. Write it out in Persian.

He ح

This is the second way to write the sound **H** in Persian. There is no difference in pronunciation between **ه** and **ح**, and both are called **He**, but using one instead of the other still counts as a misspelling.

He is the final one of the **J**aw-shaped letters in Persian. Here is a complete overview:

Shape	ح	خ	ج	چ
Letter name	He	Xe	Jim	Če
Pronounced as in...	hotel	Xavier (Spanish)	Jim	chin

✎ **9** Practise writing **He** in its four forms.

🔍 **10** Find the three **Hes** in the following paragraph.

ما حتی بولینگ بازی کردیم. خیلی
خوب بود که یک سفر طولانی
داشتم. اما حالا خوشحال هستم که
به خانه برگشتم.

📖 **11** Read the Persian letters and use the clues to work out the meaning
of the following words.

🔊 **06.03**

a Arabic names: اَحمَد – مُحَمَد – حَسَن

b Male name: نوح

c Famous scientist: اِسحاق نیوتُن

d Arab country, and the capital of a neighbour:

بَحرِین – دوحه

حِیدَرآباد

e Indian city:

🖊 **12** Here are some useful Persian words. Write them out in Persian letters based on the transliteration: **hivan** (*animal*), **mahal** (*place*)

´ayn ع

In Arabic this is a really hard-to-pronounce guttural sound, but fortunately you are learning Persian, and in Persian it is just the

#ScriptHack

´ayn looks like a mirrored lower-case **g**.

same sound as **Hamze**, that is, the sound of the stop in between 'uh-oh'. In transliteration, ´**ayn** is commonly represented as ´.

ع ـع ـعـ عـ

🖊 **13** Practise writing ´ayn in its four forms.

14 Find the two ´ayns in the following paragraph.

برای یک سال دور دنیا سفر کردم.
از آسیا شروع کردم و بعد به آفریقا،
اروپا و آمریکا سفر کردم.

15 Read the Persian letters and use the clues to work out the meaning
of the following words.

◁)) 06.04

a Countries: ‎—عَراق – عَرَبِستان سَعودی

عُمان

b Middle-Eastern politician: یاسِر عَرَفات

c Holy for Muslims: کَعبه

d Arabic names: عَلی – عُمَر

16 Here are some useful Persian words. Write them out in Persian letters based on the given transliteration: ´asal (*honey*), **abe ma´adani** (*mineral water*)

Tā ‍ط

This is a second type of **T**. In Arabic, **Tā** and **Te** are pronounced differently, but Persian has let go of this distinction while not removing the letter from the alphabet.

#ScriptHack

Tā looks like a **T** standing on its head.

It is rather uncommon though, mostly found in words and names borrowed from Arabic.

ط   ط   ط   ط

17 Practise writing **Tā** in its four forms.

🔍 **18** Find the one Tā in the following paragraph.

خیلی خوب بود که یک سفر
طولانی داشتم. اما حالا خوشحال
هستم که به خانه برگشتم.

📖 **19** Read the Persian letters and use the clues to work out the meaning of the following words.

🔊 **06.05**

a Country:

قَطَر

b Capitals of Arab nations:

مَسقَط – رَباط

c Atlantic Ocean in Persian:

اُقیانوس اَطلَس

d Famous Greek philosopher:

اَرَسطو

e Nearest star:

آلفا قِنطورِس

✏️ **20** Write the word *sultan*, which is of Arabo-Persian origin, in Persian letters. Use Tā rather than Te.

REVIEW

Here are all the letters you have learnt so far, except for diacritics:

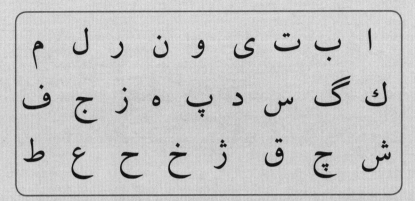

ا ب ت ی و ن ر ل
م

ك گ س د ه پ ز ج
ف

ش چ ق ژ خ ح ع
ط

🖊 1 In Persian, the alphabet is actually ordered by shapes. While you are
still missing a few letters, group the ones you have learnt by shape
and also note the names.

📖 **2** Compare the English and the Persian on these subway signs. What is the word for *line*?

خط ۱ - تجریش
Line 1-Tajrish

خط ۲ - فرهنگسرا
Line 2- Farhangsara

خط ۱ - کهریزک
Line 1- Kahrizak

خط ۲ - تهران (صادقیه)
Line 2- Tehran (adeghiyeh)

✏️ **3** Copy the Persian station names from the picture and add the missing short vowels based on the English.

7 FINISHING LINE

Ghayn غ

Ghayn looks exactly like **´ayn** except that it has a dot on top. In Persian, the pronunciation is the same as **Qe**, while Arabic distinguishes these.

#ScriptHack

Ghayn looks like a small **g** but with a dot on top. In fact, some textbooks will transliterate it as a **g** with a dot (**ġ**) but the spelling **gh** is more common.

✏️ **1** Practise writing **Ghayn** in its four forms.

🔍 **2** Find the **Ghayn** in the following paragraph.

در آفریقا، اتیوپی، موزامبیک و مصر را خیلی دوست داشتم. قاهره خیلی شلوغ بود و صحرا بسیار گرم.

LANGUAGE TIP

In Persian, many country names that end in **-ia** in English will end in **-stan**.

📖 **3** Read the Persian letters and use the clues to work out the meaning of the following words.

🔊 **07.01**

a Countries outside Europe: غَنا – اَفغانِستان

b Countries in Europe: پُرتُغال – بُلغارِستان

c US state (one word is *west*): ویرجینیای غَربی

d Savannah animal: غَزال

✏️ **4** Write the city name *Baghdad* in Persian letters.

Sād ص

This is another way to write the letter **S** in Persian. In Arabic, there is a difference in pronunciation between **Sād** and **Sin**, but in Persian they sound identical. The only reason both letters exist is because of Arabic names and words that were adopted in Persian.

#ScriptHack

Sād looks like a snake.

ضــ ـضـ ـض ض

✏ **5** Practise writing **Sād** in its four forms.

🔍 **6** Find the two **Sāds** in the following paragraph.

در آفریقا، اتیوپی، موزامبیک و مصر را خیلی دوست داشتم. قاهره خیلی شلوغ بود و صحرا بسیار گرم.

📖 **7** Read the Persian letters and use the clues to work out the meaning of the following words.
🔊 **07.02**

a Hot; dry place:
صَحرا

b Cities:
صوفیه – صَنعا

c Arabic and Persian name for Egypt:
مِصر

✏ 8 Serbia is another one of the countries that end in **-stan** in Persian. It is known as **Serbestān**. Write it in Persian.

Se ثـ

This is a third way to write the sound **S** in Persian. (In Arabic, this would be the letter **TH**, so you'll find **Se** mostly in names and words that would use **TH** in English, or in Arabic loanwords that would have that sound.)

ث ثـ ـثـ ـث

✏ 9 Practise writing **Se** in its four forms.

🔍 **10** Find the two **Ses** in the following paragraph.

اما رودخانه نیل و اهرام ثلاثه واقعاً زیبا بودند. در اروپا به موزه های زیادی رفتم. نقاشی های سالوادور دالی و وینسنت ون گوگ را دیدم.

📖 **11** Read the Persian letters and use the clues to work out the meaning of the following words.

🔊 **07.03**

a English city:

باث

b Protagonist of an English classic:

مَکبِث

c Woman's name:

اِدیث

✏️ **12** Write down the following European names in Persian: *Thelma, Thor, Judith.*

Z

There are only three letters left, which are all extremely rare in Persian (only used for Arabic loanwords) and they all sound like **Z**.

Zād

ض ضـ ـضـ ـض

Zā

ظ ظـ ـظـ ـظ

Zāl

ذ ـذ

LANGUAGE TIP

In Arabic, the first one is a kind of **D** and the other two sound like the **TH** in *that* (voiced **TH**, not unvoiced as in *thing*), transliterated as **DH**. Knowing this Arabic transliteration will help you recognize more words, but remember that in Persian, all three sound like **Z**.

🖉 **13** Practise writing **Zād**, **Zā** and **Zāl** in their four forms.

14 Find **Zād**, **Zā** and **Zāl** in the following sentence.

از آسیا شروع کردم و بعدِ به
آذربایجان، ریاض و اَبوظبی سفر
کردم.

15 Read the Persian letters and use the clues to work out the meaning
of the following words.

07.04

a Country:

آذَربایجان

b Cities:

ریاض – اَبوظبی

c A month of fasting:

رَمِضان

16 Copy the words from above.

REVIEW

Here are all the letters of the Persian alphabet, in alphabetical order now from right to left. (**Hamze** and the diacritics are not listed as part of the alphabet.)

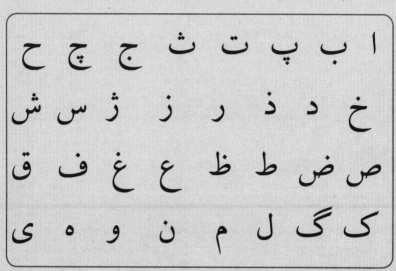

✏ **1** Write down the names of the Persian letters in alphabetical order.

✏ **2** Here's how to count from one to ten: **yek, do, se, xahār, panj, shesh, haft, hasht, noh, dah.** Write the words out in Persian.

8 EXTRA DIACRITICS AND MESHED LETTERS

This is a short lesson to cover a few more things you will encounter when reading Persian.

Lām Alef

When **Alef** follows **Lām**, the letters are not written separately, they always form a distinctive meshed shape:

لا ...لا

This shape appears relatively often, for example in the word *dollar*:

دُلار

✏ **1** Copy out the forms of **Lām Alef** and the word *dollar*.

```
_____
_ _ _ _ _ _ _ _ _ _ _ _ _ _ _ _ _ _ _
_____
_____
```

📖 **2** Read the Persian letters and use the clues to work out the meaning of the following words.

🔊 **08.01**

a Asian countries: لائوس – بَنگِلادِش – سِری‌لانکا

b American cities: آتلانتا – فیلادلفیا –
دالاس – اورلاندو –
لاس وِگاس

c African leader: نِلسون ماندِلا

d Food: سالاد – لازانیا

Tašdid

Tašdid looks like a small **w**. It is used instead of double letters in Persian. Instead of writing the same letter twice, a **Tašdid** diacritic can just be added on top. This means that the letter will audibly be pronounced twice. Like all diacritics, it is usually not written.

> **LANGUAGE TIP**
>
> There's one special thing about **Tašdid**: if a consonant carries both **Tašdid** and **Zir**, **Zir** will appear below **Tašdid**, NOT below the consonant.

Examples:

بّ	bba	بُّ	bbo	بِّ	bbe	بِ	be

This is the name *Mohammed* in Persian:

مُحَمَّد

✏️ 3 Copy the Persian word for *Mohammed* from above.

✏️ 4 Here are some useful words with **Tašdid** in Persian. Note down their pronunciation.

English	Pronunciation	Persian
child	baččе	بَچّه
pronunciation		تَلَفُّظ
vowel		مُصَوَّت
valley		دَرّه
alive		حَیّ

Tanvin

When a word ends in **-an** or **-en** in Persian, you may find that this ending is written not with **Nun** but with a double **Zebar** (two lines instead of one).

In Arabic, there are also **Tanvin** for the other vowel diacritics. They always appear at the end of a word and they mean that the word does not end in the vowel but in **-n**.

> **LANGUAGE TIP**
>
> When the **-en** ending occurs in Persian, it is almost always an adverb – a word that would end in *-ly* in English. In Arabic, the **Tanvin** are also used for other types of words.

🖊 **5 Here are some useful words with Tanvin in Persian. Note down their pronunciation.**

English	Pronunciation	Persian
really		حَقیقَتاً
quickly		سَریعاً
for example		مَثَلاً
actually		واقِعاً

REVIEW

📖 1 Read the Persian letters and use the clues to work out the meaning of the following words.

a Countries:

فَنلاند – وِنِزوِئلا –
گواتِمالا

b Cities:

آدِلاید – گِلاسگو –
دارُالسَلام – اِسلامآباد –
کازابِلانکا – میلان

c Metal:

پِلاتین

d Religion:

اِسلام

✏️ 2 Which of the cities would you like to travel to? Copy their names.

3 Here are some useful words in Persian. Note down their pronunciation.

English	Pronunciation	Persian
firstly		اوّلاً
seriously		جدّاً

9 NUMBERS

English and other European languages - indeed most of the world's languages - use what are known as Western Arabic numerals, which originally came from India, Persia and Mesopotamia. However, Persia adopted numerals that originated in North Africa. These Persian numerals are widely used in Iran, for example on car number plates, bank notes or metro signs. It is therefore quite useful to be able to read them. They resemble the traditional Arabic numerals but the shape of the 4, 5 and 6 are different.

۱	۲	۳	۴	۵
1	2	3	4	5
۶	۷	۸	۹	۰
6	7	8	9	0

LANGUAGE TIP
Pay particular attention to the difference between the Persian numerals for 6 and 9.

The use of these numerals is the same as in the Western system, i.e. to write the number 30 one would write ۳ and then ۰, and the number 506 is ۵۰۶. Notice that the numbers are even read left to right, just like in English.

📖 1 Read the following Persian numbers:

۲, ۷, ۱۵, ۸۹, ۲۰۰, ۹۰۲

📖 **2** How many Iranian Rial is this bank note worth?

📖 **3** Write the following numbers in Persian: 42, 50, 66, 700, 2033.

REVIEW

1 Read the number on this Iranian taxi's number plate.

2 Write down your phone number in Persian.

LANGUAGE TIP

For extra practice, fill an entire practice page at the end of this course with the Persian phone numbers of your friends and family.

Congratulations, you have reached the end of this course!

To be able to read Persian novels or newspapers, you will still have to learn the language itself. However, you can already do a lot. Check the things you can do:

- [ ] I can read and pronounce the Persian alphabet.

- [ ] I can read the names of streets or shops.

- [ ] I can read people's names on their business cards.

- [ ] I know where to ring when visiting Persian-speaking friends.

- [ ] I can recognize brands when shopping.

- [ ] I can spot English words when they masquerade as Persian.

ANSWER KEY

Lesson 1

2

براى يک سال دور دنيا سفر کردم.
از آسيا شروع کردم و بعد به آفريقا،
اروپا و آمريکا سفر کردم. در آسيا
کشورهاى اندونزى ، ويتنام، چين،
کره و ژاپن را خيلى دوست داشتم.

5 a nānā *Nana*

 b Ānā *Anna*

7

براى يک سال دور دنيا سفر کردم.
از آسيا شروع کردم و بعد به آفريقا،
اروپا و آمريکا سفر کردم. در آسيا
کشور هاى اندونزى، ويتنام، چين
کره و ژاپن را خيلى دوست داشتم.

8 a āy! *Hey!*

 b Āni *Annie, Nina*

10
برای یک سال دور دنیا سفر کردم.
از آسیا شروع کردم و بعد به آفریقا،
اروپا و آمریکا سفر کردم.

11 a *Ivan*

   b vini *Winnie*

   c *Yuan*

   d āyuva *Iowa*

14
در آسیا کشورهای اندونزی،
ویتنام، چین، کره و ژاپن را خیلی
دوست داشتم.

15 a **vitni** *Whitney*, **Āntuniu** *Antonio*

   b yuta *Utah*, **tāyvān** *Taiwan*

   c at *(@)*

Review

2 *Tony*

3

Persian	Transliteration	Meaning
تو	**tu**	*you*
آن	**ān**	*that*
تا	**tā**	*until*

Lesson 2

From now on, the answers will skip the transliteration except if the Persian spelling is quite different from the English.

2 قاهره خیلی شلوغ بود و صحرا بسیار گرم. اما رودخانه نیل و اهرام ثلاثه واقعاً زیبا بودند.

3 a **ālu** *Hello*

b **Itāliā** *Italy*, **Lituāni** *Lithuania*

c *Tallinn*, **liun** *Lyon*

d *Nile*

e **Luti** *Lotti*

8 در آسیا کشورهای اندونزی، ویتنام، چین، کره و ژاپن را خیلی دوست داشتم. سوشی و چای ژاپنی خیلی خوشمزه بود! در آفریقا، اتیوپی، موزامبیک و مصر را خیلی دوست داشتم.

9 a *Tim*, **Tām** *Tom*, *William*

b **Malt** *Malta*, *Mali*

c *Lima*, **Manil** *Manila*

d *aluminium*, *lithium*, *titanium*

e **miliun** *million*, *vitamin*

11 a Ena *Anna, Eva*

b neyten *Nathan, Alan,* **iten** *Ethan*

c *Yen*

d *Vietnam*

e Nānet *Nantes,* **āten** *Athens*

f *Lenin*

13 برای یک سال دور دنیا سفر کردم.
از آسیا شروع کردم و بعد به آفریقا،
اروپا و آمریکا سفر کردم.

14 a *Maria, Marie, Mary*

b *Ruth, Terry*

c *Marilyn Monroe*

d *internet*

e *Turin, Tirana,* **turentu** *Toronto, Montreal*

f rumāni *Romania,* **muritāni** *Mauritania, Iran*

16 در آفریقا، اتیوپی، موزامبیک و
مصر را خیلی دوست داشتم. قاهره
خیلی شلوغ بود و صحرا بسیار گرم.
اما رودخانه نیل و اهرام ثلاثه واقعاً
زیبا بودند.

17 a *bar*

b *Barbara, Benjamin, Benny, Betty, Bill,* **berāyān** *Brian,* **rābert** *Robert*

c *Melbourne, Berlin, Baltimore,* **bulunyā** *Bologna, Beirut, Nairobi*

d **beritānya** *Britain,* **albani** *Albania, Benin, Namibia*

e **bāb marli** *Bob Marley*

Review

2 *Ruth, William, Lena, Ben, Billy, Maria, Terry, Baron*

تِری، اِلِن بِنیامین ₃

Lesson 3

₂ برای یک سال دور دنیا سفر کردم.
از آسیا شروع کردم و بعد به آفریقا،
اروپا و آمریکا سفر کردم.

3 a **kātrin** *Catherine, Carmen, Monica,* **māyk** *Mike,* **māykel** *Michael*

b *Kenya, Cuba, Cameroon, Monaco, Ukraine*

c *Tokyo, Bangkok,* **kitu** *Quito, Canberra,* **nyu yurk** *New York, Ankara*

d **kari** *curry, kiwi,* **muka** *mocha*

e **bil kelintun** *Bill Clinton, Barack Obama*

f **tālkin** *Tolkien, Mark Twain*

g *nickel, bacteria, caricature,* **elekteruniki** *electronic, kilometre*

مارک، کیم، کِوین ₄

چیزهای زیادی درباره تولستوی، ۶

شکسپیر، گوته، شیلر و کارل مارکس

یادگرفتم. به موسیقی موتزارت،

باخ و چایکوفسکی گوش کردم.

7 a tennis, **beysbāl** baseball, **buks** boxing

  b eskā ska, salsa

  c Boris, **estiven** Stephen

  d Keats, Sartre, Tolstoy

  e Lisbon, Istanbul, Barcelona, **beristul** Bristol, **nyukasel** Newcastle, Valencia

  f Siberia, Assam, Asia

سامبا، تاکسی، ویروس ۸

برای یک سال دور دنیا سفر کردم. ۱۰

از آسیا شروع کردم و بعد به آفریقا،

اروپا و آمریکا سفر کردم. در آسیا

کشورهای اندونزی، ویتنام، چین،

کره و ژاپن را خیلی دوست داشتم.

11 a *Canada, Bermuda, Sudan, Denmark, Andorra, Rwanda, Ecuador*

   b *Sydney, Madrid, Amsterdam, Dublin, Rotterdam*

   c *Alexander, Cindy, Dimitri, Eddy, Edward*

   d *Celine Dion, Bob Dylan*

   e *Indie, drama*

12 رادیو، لیموناد، دِموکرات

14 a *Don, Odin,* **odri** *Audrey,* **borus** *Bruce, Oscar, Otto*

   b *Oslo, Rome, Moscow, Ottawa, Kabul, Omsk*

   c **ostorālia** *Australia, Colombia, Botswana, Samoa*

   d *sodium, cobalt,* **borom** *bromine,* **yod** *iodine, uranium*

   e **otubus** *autobus*

15 دُکتُر، کُمِدی

17 نقاشی های سالوادور دالی و وینسنت ون گوگ را دیدم. چیزهای زیادی درباره تولستوی، شکسپیر، گوته، شیلر و کارل مارکس یادگرفتم.

18 a *Olga, Oleg, Yevgeni*

   b *Congo, Uganda, Madagascar, Senegal*

   c **engelestan**

   d *Kingston, Belgrade, Edinburgh, Riga, Wellington, Santiago*

   e *Gautama Buddha, Martin Luther King, Gandhi*

   f **buling** *bowling, guitar, yoga,* **regey** *reggae*

Review

2 āb

3 اراک، کِرمان، ساری، گُرگان

Lesson 4

2 در آسیا کشورهای اندونزی، ویتنام، چین، کره و ژاپن را خیلی دوست داشتم. سوشی و چای ژاپنی خیلی خوشمزه بود! در آفریقا، اتیوپی، موزامبیک و مصر را خیلی دوست داشتم.

3 a *pasta, papaya*

   b *Pakistan, Peru, Nepal, Panama,* **espānya** *Spain* (*España*)

   c *Paris, Prague, Budapest, Porto, Antwerp, Liverpool*

   d *Minneapolis, Tampa,* **pitesberg** *Pittsburgh, Indianapolis, Winnipeg*

   e **kupernik** *Copernicus, Kepler*

   f *Neptune, Pluto*

   g *park, opera, diplomacy*

4 پُل، پیتِر، پیر

6 a *Adam, Adrian, Agnes, Pat, Matt*

b landan *London, Auckland, Vancouver, Portland, Calgary, Cleveland, Aberdeen, Birmingham*

c *Thailand, Ireland, Yemen, Singapore, Iceland, Turkmenistan*

d *rap,* **alkol** *alcohol, atom, kilogram,* **tanbāku** *tobacco*

7 بَتمَن، سوپِرمَن

12 چیزهای زیادی درباره تولستوی، شکسپیر، گوته، شیلر و کارل مارکس یادگرفتم. به موسیقی موتزارت، باخ و چایکوفسکی گوش کردم.

13 a *haha, aha*

b *Houdini, Harry Potter*

c *Russia,* **torkie** *Turkey,* **surie** *Syria, Holland, Honduras*

d *(The) Bahamas, Hawaii*

e *Hong Kong, Taipei,* **dehli nu** *New Delhi, Hanoi, Agra*

f *Helsinki, Copenhagen, Hamburg, Stockholm*

g *Hannah, Helen*

14 هُتِل، کُنگِره، هَمبِرگِر، مِناره، کاراته

در آسیا کشورهای اندونزی، ویتنام، ۱۶
چین، کره و ژاپن را خیلی دوست
داشتم. سوشی و چای ژاپنی خیلی
خوشمزه بود! در آفریقا، اتیوپی،
موزامبیک و مصر را خیلی دوست
داشتم.

17 a berezil *Brazil,* **nyu ziland** *New Zealand,* **andunezi** *Indonesia,*
Uzbekistan, Zimbabwe, Mozambique

b *Mexico City, Zagreb, Basel,* **berizben** *Brisbane, San (Saint)*
Petersburg

c lidz *Leeds,* **velz** *Wales,* **teymz** *Thames*

d bitelz *Beatles, Walt Disney*

e *pizza, bazaar, diesel,* **susyālizm** *socialism, television*

سوزی، سوزان، لیزا، زَکَری، اِلِیزابِت ۱۸

به موسیقی موتزارت، باخ و ۲۰
چایکوفسکی گوش کردم. در آمریکا
با دوستم، مارک از یک ساحل به
ساحل دیگر سفر کردیم. از ایالات

بسیاری دیدار کردیم. مثل
نیویورک، نیو همشایر، ماساچوست،
ویرجینیا، نیوجرزی و اوکلاهوما.
تکیلا و ویسکی نوشیدیم و دوستان
جدید پیدا کردیم.

21 a *Gina, Angie,* **jorj** *George, Jack,* **jeymz** *James, Jenny, Judy, Julia*

    b *Jakarta, Los Angeles, Nanjing*

    c *Nigeria,* **kambuj** *Cambodia, Tajikistan, Djibouti*

    d **jurjia** *Georgia,* **nyu jersi** *New Jersey, Virginia*

    e *Jimi Hendrix, Mick Jagger, John Lennon*

22 جاز، جودو، نینجا، جین

Review

2 *Darjeeling*

3 کِلیمانجارو، هیمالیا، گِرینلَند

Lesson 5

2 برای یک سال دور دنیا سفر کردم.
از آسیا شروع کردم و بعد به آفریقا،
اروپا و آمریکا سفر کردم.

3 a *Cardiff, Belfast,* **āksfurd** *Oxford, Halifax*

  b *California, Florida, Philippines,* **faranse** *France, Fiji*

  c *San Francisco, Dusseldorf, Frankfurt, Hannover*

  d **zigmund feruid** *Siegmund Freud, Kafka*

  e **wayfay** *Wi-Fi*

4 فیلم، گُلف، تِلِفُن

6 a *Haiti, Israel,* **pārāgueh** *Paraguay, Jamaica*

  b **Bu'nus āyres** *Buenos Aires, Sao Paulo, Macao,* **nyu urle'ān** *New Orleans*

  c *Naomi, Manuel, Paulo, Leonardo*

  d *neon, theatre, video*

7 ناپلئون، کِلُئوپاترا

9 مثل نیویورک، نیو همشایر، ماساچوست، ویرجینیا، نیوجرزی و اوکلاهوما. تکیلا و ویسکی نوشیدیم و دوستان جدید پیدا کردیم. خیلی خوش گذشت.

10 a *Natasha, Patricia, Masha*

  b *Washington, Shanghai, Chicago,* **eshtutgārt** *Stuttgart, Nashville*

  c **Shekspier** *Shakespeare, Schiller, Pushkin*

  d *machine, rickshaw, shah, sushi*

شیلی، اُتریش، مَراکِش **11**

در آسیا کشورهای اندونزی، ویتنام، **13**
چین، کره و ژاپن را خیلی دوست
داشتم. سوشی و چای ژاپنی خیلی
خوشمزه بود!

14 a *Charles, Richard*

  b *Manchester, Richmond, Rochester, Chengdu, Chennai, Karachi*

  c *Massachusetts, Chad,* **chek** *Czech (Republic), China*

  d *Leonardo da Vinci, Tchaikovsky*

  e *Winston Churchill*

  f *Cherokee, Apache*

چای، تای چی، لیچی **15**

در آفریقا، اتیوپی، موزامبیک و مصررا **17**
خیلی دوست داشتم. قاهره خیلی شلوغ
بود و صحرا بسیار گرم. اما رودخانه
نیل و اهرام ثلاثه واقعا زیبا بودند.

18 a *Qur'an*

   b *Africa*

   c *Macedonia, Kazakhstan, Kirghizstan*

   d musiqi *music*

19 قَهوه

Review

3 کاشان، قُم، تهران اِصفَهان

Lesson 6

2 در آسیا کشورهای اندونزی، ویتنام، چین، کره و ژاپن را خیلی دوست داشتم. سوشی و چای ژاپنی خیلی خوشمزه بود!

3 a *Japan, Argentina*

   b *Johannesburg, Geneva, Rio de Janeiro, Shenzhen*

   c *Julius Caesar*

   d *nitrogen, hydrogen, oxygen*

   e *garage*

   f *tragedy*

4 بِلژیک، نُروژ

در آسیا کشورهای اندونزی، ویتنام، چین، کره و ژاپن را ▮خیلی▮ دوست داشتم. سوشی و چای ژاپنی ▮خیلی▮ ▮خوشمزه▮ بود! در آفریقا، اتیوپی، موزامبیک و مصر را ▮خیلی▮ دوست داشتم.

7 **a** xāled Khalid

b Zurich, Bucharest, Munich, Utrecht, San José, San Juan

c Bach

d Chekhov

8 خَلیفه

10

ما ▮حتی▮ بولینگ بازی کردیم. خیلی خوب بود که یک سفر طولانی داشتم. اما ▮حالا▮ خوشحال هستم که به خانه برگشتم.

11 **a** Ahmed, Muhammad, Hassan

b **Nuh** Noah

c **ishaq nyutun** Isaac Newton

d Bahrain, Doha

e Hyderabad

12 حِیوان، مَحَل

14
برای یک سال دور دنیا سفر کردم.
از آسیا شروع کردم و بعد به آفریقا،
اروپا و آمریکا سفر کردم.

15 a Iraq, ´arabestan sa´udi Saudi Arabia, Oman

b Yasser Arafat

c Ka'bah

d Ali, Omar

16 عَسَل، آب مَعَدَنی

18
خیلی خوب بود که یک سفر
طولانی داشتم. اما حالا خوشحال
هستم که به خانه برگشتم.

19 a Qatar

b Muscat, Rabat

c **Oqiānus** Atlas

d **Arastu** Aristotle

e Alpha Centauri

سُلطان 20

Review

خط 2

تَجریش 3

فَرَهَنگَسَرا

کهریزک

تِهران (صادِقیه)

Lesson 7

در آفریقا، اتیوپی، موزامبیک و 2
مصر را خیلی دوست داشتم. قاهره
خیلی شلوغ بود و صحرا بسیار گرم.

3 a *Ghana, Afghanistan*

b *Portugal, Bulgaria*

c *(West) Virginia* (**gharbi**)

d *gazelle*

4 بَغداد

6 در آفریقا، اتیوپی، موزامبیک و مصر را خیلی دوست داشتم. قاهره خیلی شلوغ بود و صحرا بسیار گرم.

7 **a** *Sahara*

　　b *Sofia, Sana´a*

　　c **Mesr**

8 صِربِستان

10 اما رودخانه نیل و اهرام ثلا ثه واقعاً زیبا بودند. در اروپا به موزه های زیادی رفتم. نقاشی های سالوادور دالی و وینسنت ون گوگ را دیدم.

11 **a** *Bath*

　　b *Macbeth*

　　c *Edith*

12 تُلما، تُر، جودیت

از آسیا شروع کردم و بعد به
آذَربایجان، ریاض و اَبوظَبی سفر
کردم.

15 a *Azerbaijan*

   b *Riyadh, Abu Dhabi*

   c *Ramadan*

Review

2

یَک، دو، سه، چَهار، پَنج، شِش،
هَفت، هَشت، نُه، دَه

Lesson 8

2 **a** *Laos, Bangladesh, Sri Lanka*

   b *Atlanta, Philadelphia, Dallas, Orlando, Las Vegas*

   c *Nelson Mandela*

   d *salad,* **lazagnya** *lasagne*

4

English	Pronunciation	Persian
child	**bačče**	بَچّه
pronunciation	**talaffoz**	تَلَفُّظ
vowel	**mosavvat**	مُصَوَّت
valley	**darre**	دَرّه
alive	**hayy**	حَیّ

5

English	Pronunciation	Persian
really	**haqiqatan**	حَقیقَتاً
quickly	**sariʹan**	سَریعاً
for example	**masalan**	مَثَلاً
actually	**vāqeʹan**	واقِعاً

Review

1 a *Finland, Venezuela, Guatemala*

   b *Adelaide, Glasgow, Dar es Salaam, Islamabad, Casablanca, Milan*

   c *platinum*

   d *Islam*

English	Pronunciation	Persian
firstly	**avvalan**	اوَّلاً
seriously	**jeddan**	جِدّاً

Lesson 9

1 The numbers are: 2, 7, 15, 89, 200, 902.

2 It's a 50,000 Rial note.

3 ۴۲، ۵۰، ۶۶، ۷۰۰، ۲۰۳۳

Review

1 The taxi's number plate says 23 T 278 33.

PHRASEBOOK

🔊 10.01

Hello	**Dorud**	دُرود
Good morning	**Bāmdād xuš**	بامداد خوش
Good evening	**Asr xuš**	عَصر خوش
Good night	**Šab xuš**	شَب خوش
Welcome	**Xuš āmadid**	خوش آمَدید
How are you? (formal)	**Xubid?**	خوبید؟
Fine, thank you	**Xubam, sepās**	خوبَم/ سِپاس
Nice to meet you	**Xušvaqtam**	خوشوَقتَم
Please/You're welcome	**Xvāheš mikonam**	خواهِش میکُنَم
Thanks	**Sepās**	سِپاس
Sorry	**Bebaxšid**	بِبَخشید
How do you say ... in Persian?	**Shoma ... ru be Fārsi chi migin?**	شُما ... رو به فارسی چی میگین؟
I don't understand	**Nemifahmam**	نِمیفَهمَم
Yes/No	**Āre/Nah**	آره / نَه
Goodbye	**Xodā negahdār**	خُدانِگَهدار

PHOTO CREDITS

p 45 © aquatarkus / Shutterstock.com

p 72 © Rolf G Wackenberg / Shutterstock.com

p 84 © Rolf G Wackenberg / Shutterstock.com

p 100 © Anton_Ivanov / Shutterstock.com

p 101 © C. Na Songkhla / Shutterstock.com